Healing the Impossible

RECLAIMING YOUR DESTINY
AFTER ABORTION LOSS

Pam Thompson

TRILOGY CHRISTIAN PUBLISHERS
Tustin, CA

Trilogy Christian Publishers
A Wholly Owned Subsidiary of Trinity Broadcasting Network
2442 Michelle Drive
Tustin, CA 92780

Healing the Impossible

Copyright © 2024 by Pam Thompson

Scripture quotations marked KJV are taken from the King James Version of the Bible. Public domain.

All Scriptures quotations marked CEV are taken from The Holy Bible, Contemporary English Version: Scripture quotations marked CEV are from the Contemporary English Version Copyright © 1991, 1992, 1995 by American Bible Society. Used by Permission.

Scripture quotations marked TPT are from The Passion Translation®. Copyright © 2017, 2018, 2020 by Passion & Fire Ministries, Inc. Used by permission. All rights reserved. ThePassionTranslation.com.

Scripture quotations are from the ESV® Bible (The Holy Bible, English Standard Version®), © 2001 by Crossway, a publishing ministry of Good News Publishers. Used by permission. All rights reserved. The ESV text may not be quoted in any publication made available to the public by a Creative Commons license. The ESV may not be translated in whole or in part into any other language.

Scripture quotations marked GW. GOD'S WORD© translation © 1995, 2003, 2013, 2014, 2019, 2020 by God's Word to the Nations Mission Society; used with permission.

Scriptures marked Scripture quotations marked (NLT) are taken from the Holy Bible, New Living Translation, copyright ©1996, 2004, 2015 by Tyndale House Foundation. Used by permission of Tyndale House Publishers, Carol Stream, Illinois 60188. All rights reserved.

The Voice Scripture (VOICE) taken from The Voice™. Copyright © 2012 by Ecclesia Bible Society. Used by permission. All rights reserved.

Scripture quotations taken from the NASB2020® New American Standard Bible®, Copyright © 2020 Copyright by The Lockman Foundation. Used by permission. All rights reserved. lockman.org

Scripture taken from the New King James Version® (NKJV). Copyright © 1982 by Thomas Nelson. Used by permission. All rights reserved.

Scripture quotations marked (NIV) are taken from the Holy Bible, New International Version®, NIV®. Copyright © 1973, 1978, 1984, 2011 by Biblica, Inc.™ Used by permission of Zondervan. All rights reserved worldwide. www.zondervan.comThe "NIV" and "New International Version" are trademarks registered in the United States Patent and Trademark Office by Biblica, Inc.™

All rights reserved, including the right to reproduce this book or portions thereof in any form whatsoever.

For information, address Trilogy Christian Publishing
Rights Department, 2442 Michelle Drive, Tustin, Ca 92780.

Trilogy Christian Publishing/ TBN and colophon are trademarks of Trinity Broadcasting Network.

For information about special discounts for bulk purchases, please contact Trilogy Christian Publishing.

Trilogy Disclaimer: The views and content expressed in this book are those of the author and may not necessarily reflect the views and doctrine of Trilogy Christian Publishing or the Trinity Broadcasting Network.

10 9 8 7 6 5 4 3 2 1

Library of Congress Cataloging-in-Publication Data is available.

ISBN 979-8-89333-892-8

ISBN 979-8-89333-893-5 (ebook)

This book is dedicated to women like me who have been wounded by abortion. May this book help you in your own journey toward inner healing, restoration and your true destiny.

Preface

In our distractable culture, it's so easy to bury our abortions. Just do it and go on, but that's not as easy as it sounds.

In my 20's, I had an abortion. I thought I could do it, and it would be done. I never thought I would carry it around like baggage.

I thought I could have an abortion and my life would continue as I knew it, but that wasn't the case. After the procedure, it seemed like something in me had changed. The joyful, full-of-life person I was became more of an act. My abortion haunted me with sadness and shame. I didn't understand. Where were these feelings coming from? I thought I'd have an abortion, and it would be all over like nothing happened. Now, I was dealing with emotions I didn't expect: guilt, shame, regret, anger, sorrow, and the "what ifs."

I tried to share it with a friend once, but I decided at the last minute not to share. I didn't want to take the chance that they would tell someone else. And you know, we all tell someone else.

As a result, I kept my secret hidden for over 20 years, living in fear of judgment and rejection. I was terrified that someone would find out and I'd be labeled.

Post-abortion grief is often not recognized and is a difficult thing to talk about. It's hard to talk about because no one is talking about it. People are so set in their viewpoints that the woman who is suffering after an abortion, regardless of her perspective, is lost in the mix and, more often than not, goes on without help or support.

Some studies report post-abortion effects or side effects, while other studies find no association with post-abortion side effects. Is this a situation where the results align with the views of the researchers? Who knows? Who cares?

Forget the viewpoints, forget the research that argues one side or the other, and just focus on yourself. Are you experiencing feelings of anxiety or guilt? Do you feel agitated or sad? Feelings that you may not have felt prior to your abortion(s) and now seem to be weighing you down? I know those feelings all too well.

It wasn't until a trusted friend noticed something was off with me that I finally found the courage to open up. Sharing my pain was a turning point, which led me to the healing that I never realized I needed.

This book is for all the women out there who, like me, have been scarred by abortion. Know you are not alone. Statistics* show that many women have walked a similar path, carrying the weight of their choices in silence. It's time to break free from the chains of shame and guilt.

On these pages, I share my healing journey, offering stories and reflections of my own life to help guide you on your own path of healing and restoration.

Know that as you pour out your thoughts and feelings on the journal pages, you are not alone. My heart is with you as you let go of the past and embrace a future filled with hope and restoration.

Introduction
How to Use This Book

Consider this book a personal healing journey. In it, I mention God and refer to quotes from various translations of the Bible. If you don't believe in God, don't let that stop you; read the book anyway. I believe you'll be better for it.

At the end of each chapter, you will be encouraged to pray, take action, and speak out an affirmation.

"Wait, what? Pray? Action? Affirmation? What's that about?"

Pray: Praying is simply a conversation with God. If you're asking: "What if I don't believe in God"? Well, I'll say, don't let the mention of 'God' or 'prayer' stop you. Keep an open mind. If you're still struggling with stress, anger, or anxiety over your past abortion choices, what do you have to lose?

The Bible verses are there to inspire hope. The Bible is thousands of years old and has stood the test of time.

Many people believe it is the inspired written word of God. Don't worry if you don't believe this; just consider the verse's age-old wisdom words.

Action: Journaling will be an important tool as you work through this book to help you make sense of how and why you're feeling. A 2018 study* found evidence that journaling can help reduce symptoms of depression, anxiety, and anger. It will also help you to recognize and understand your triggers, which we will discuss later. Additional benefits of journaling are that it boosts emotional intelligence, encourages self-confidence, and stimulates creativity. Don't consider Journaling as hard work but as a part of your healing journey. It's a win.

Affirmation: An affirmation is a positive statement about yourself.

Speak the affirmations out loud. When you speak an affirmation out loud, you are speaking a positive statement of who you are and who you want to become. Positive affirmations can influence our behaviors and habits and can even rewire our brains to think positively and drive back negative thoughts. When you speak an affirmation out loud, you will hear yourself speaking; hearing your voice will help you believe it.

Affirmations are powerful. Refer to them often until they are embedded in your mind and heart.

When you read this book, consider finding a place to be alone to read the prayers and affirmations out loud.

Then, when it comes time to journal, you will more clearly understand your feelings and be able to express them.

In this book, I am sharing my own personal experiences and opinions with you, and I am not a doctor or medical practitioner. Many of the issues outlined in this book can be highly complex. Don't hesitate to reach out to your doctor or healthcare specialist for help.

Contents

Prologue | *Where It Began* xv

Block 1

Shock 7

Relief? 13

Memory 19

Anger 25

Numb 31

Triggers 37

Wounded 43

Stuck 49

Shame 55

Premeditated 61

Guilt 67

What If? 73

Grief 79

God? 85

Ask 91

Courage 97

Forgiveness 103

Forgive 109

Forgive Myself 115

Hello	121
Heaven	127
Letter	133
Mail	139
Grace	145
Hope	151
Purpose	157
Share	163
New Life	169
Pursue	175
Thankful	181
Restoration	185
Afterword | *God Is Our Natural Environment*	191
Journal Prompts	193
Acknowledgments	197
References	199
About the Author	201

Prologue
Where It Began

The sun was shining in the restaurant bringing a sense of warmth on a cold winter day in January.

Nancy and I met in the parking lot and walked in the door together. I was excited to meet Nancy for breakfast. Meeting a friend for breakfast was always a thing I loved to do, and this day was no different. We were greeted with a smile and were quickly guided to a booth for two. We usually sat in a booth or at a table for four, but today, we were given a small booth that sat just the two of us.

Our conversation went rolling along, just like our other breakfast get-togethers. Meeting Nancy always meant we'd chew up the meaty subjects with no topic off the table, and this day was no exception.

I didn't know at that point just how this morning's conversation would change the entire direction of my life.

Our meals came to the table, and we paused momentarily to take a bite or two between our discussion topics.

Suddenly, Nancy stopped, placed her arms on the table with utensils in each hand, looked up at me, and asked a question I wasn't expecting,

"What's the plug, Pam? Where's the block?"

Block

"Where's the block, Pam?" asked my friend Nancy while we were out for breakfast one cold Friday morning. Her question came out of the blue and stopped me in my tracks. Everything I was just thinking left my mind. My immediate reaction was to drop my head, chin to chest. As my head went down, my hands went up to cover my face. All I could see in my mind's eye was the word ABORTION. It was lit up like a marquee billboard on Broadway. ABORTION.

For over 20 years, I never told anyone I had an abortion. It was a secret I never thought I'd share. Sitting across from Nancy with my head down, I silently prayed. "God, is this it? Do you want me to tell Nancy what I did?"

Somehow, I knew I had to tell her. So, fearful and anxious, I told Nancy. She immediately prayed for me and said, "God has forgiven you, Pam, but you need healing."

My healing journey began that day.

Do you feel blocked? Is there something in your way that is stopping you from going forward? Something that keeps gnawing at your head and heart? It's time to give it up and let it go.

> *So, we must get rid of everything that slows us down, especially the sin that just won't let go. And we must be determined to run the race that is ahead of us.*
> -Hebrews 12:1b-2 (CEV)

Prayer

Are you there, God? It's me. I just want to know You're there, and I am asking that You help me get unblocked, that You would lead me to healing and wholeness. Help me drop the weight I've been carrying. Thank You.

Action

Begin today to capture your thoughts on the journal pages as you work your way through this book. The amount of healing you receive will be directly related to the work you put in. It's a self-guided journey, so give it all you got, and you won't regret it. You will find some journaling prompts at the back of the book to help you journal. Below are a few suggestions to get you started. Choose one or as many as you like.

- As I begin my personal healing journey, I am feeling...
- The thing that made me pick up this book was...
- When I have completed this journey, I want to feel...

Affirmation

Today, I begin my healing journey. I will make peace with my past and let go of everything that weighs me down.

"As long as you're alive, you always have a chance to start again."

-Emily Acker

JOURNAL

_____
_____
_____
_____
_____
_____
_____
_____

HEALING THE IMPOSSIBLE

Shock

This doesn't make sense; how did I get here?

I believed them when they told me it was my right. I believed them when they told me it was my body and my choice, but yet now here I am, and I'm in shock. I'm in shock because I can't seem to forget. I can't get it out of my head. A sense of guilt hangs over me that wasn't there before.

I don't want to go to a baby shower, let alone talk about babies. Where have all these negative feelings come from? It is like a dark cloud came over me and dumped its blackness on me. Shame is like a shadow I cast everywhere I go. What's this sense of sadness that I seem to now carry? It's unfamiliar, but why? A grief has come over me that I never expected. Shouldn't I be feeling relief right now? What's that all about? Where is it coming from?

When I chose abortion, I was left with feelings I didn't expect. I was left feeling stunned, sad, and mad, and I didn't understand WHY? I thought I could do this, and it would be done. Yet, I was left with this feeling that my choice was so much bigger than just me. The implications were beyond me and out of my control. What was that all about?

Are you in shock? Are you surprised that you're carrying a heaviness that wasn't there before? Maybe you're feeling wounded or hardened. Does your bright and happy attitude now seem like an act? Or maybe you feel a little more critical or cynical than before?

Choosing not to talk about it hasn't made it go away. You don't have to stay there.

> *He's (the devil) been a murderer right from the start! He never stood with the truth, for he's full of nothing but lies-lying is his native tongue.*
> -John 8:44 (TPT)

Prayer

Dear God, you see me where I am, and where I am is a place of confusion. I thought I made the right choice, but my heart is disturbed, and I'm hurt. God, I ask for Your help. Help me out of this dark place I have unintentionally put myself into.

Action

Write the areas you need healing. Now close your eyes and see yourself handing your list to God, and pray "God, I give all my hurt and pain to you, help."

Affirmation

I will walk in perfect peace. I'm not fearful but courageous.

"Peace begins with a smile."

-Mother Teresa

JOURNAL

Relief?

I walked out of the building with a sense of relief. A sense of relief that it was over. That sense of relief only lasted a few steps. As I walked towards the waiting car, I felt empty. Relief was gone and was now being replaced with a sense of sadness. What had I just done? I felt like a piece of me was gone. I felt like a shell of who I once was, and like I was leaving a big part of myself behind.

I tried to push that reality out of my head. I tried to feel happy it was done and hoped nothing had changed.

I concentrated on my every step. I was looking down, but something caused me to look up. As I walked toward the waiting car, I looked up because it had begun to snow. Large white fluffy flakes were gently falling from the dark sky.

I reached the car, got in, and we drove away. I don't recall any conversation in the car, just silence as I watched the falling snow. I didn't want to think about the day. I wanted to simply forget it all. Little did I know that everything in my life would change that day.

Did you feel a sense of relief? Maybe you felt no relief after your abortion experience, or perhaps it was short-lived like mine, or maybe, in some ways, you still feel relief. Know that God was with you. He was at your side as you signed the papers and waited for the procedure. He was beside you, holding your hand as you went through it. You may not have felt His presence, but He was there.

> *Where could I go from Your Spirit? Where could I run and hide from Your face? If I go up to heaven, you're there! If I go down to the realm of the dead, You're there too!*
> -Psalm 139:7-8 (TPT)

Prayer

Dear God, Thank You. Even if I didn't know it, You were with me through the whole thing. And thank You for being here with me now. Help me get through this book, finish it, and finish well.

Action

Use your imagination and write a story about you and God spending an afternoon together or having coffee at a café. What would you like to say to Him? What do you think He'd like to say to you?

Affirmation

God Himself goes before me and never leaves me, so I'm never fearful or anxious.

"No one can pray and worry at the same time."
-Max Lucado

JOURNAL

Memory

"My body, my choice." If that's true, why is this still hanging over me? Why can't I just forget? Why am I still dealing with this?

My friend Debbie said it perfectly when she said: "I don't think about my appendix, but I can't seem to forget my child."

The argument of "My body, my choice" no longer holds water for me. Somehow, I knew that whether I chose to admit it or deny it, I had ended a life. The little clump of cells had its own set of DNA, not my DNA, its own set. That's the science. We were two separate people.

Did you know our physical bodies know and suffer trauma from pregnancy loss? There is a cellular connection between every mother and child. It's a biological phenomenon known as microchimerism. We'll talk more about this a little later.

Have you struggled with your decision? Is your head telling you you've made the right choice, yet your heart can't make that connection and is trying to tell you something else?

> *If we say we have not sinned, we are fooling ourselves, and the truth isn't in our hearts. But if we confess our sins to God, he can always be trusted to forgive us and take our sins away.*
> *-1 John 1:8-9 (CEV)*

Prayer

Dear God, I feel disjointed or fragmented, like there is a rift between my head and heart. Help me to reconnect my head and my heart.

Action

Reflect on how the biases you hold have shaped your decisions. What bias would you like to shift? Journal your thoughts.

Affirmation

I cry out to God, and He hears and restores me.

"Storms make the oak grow deeper roots."
-George Hebert

JOURNAL

HEALING THE IMPOSSIBLE

Anger

No one told me about the potential side effects of abortion—nothing, not even a whisper. When I made the call to inquire about the abortion procedure, I was pushed through the whole system as fast as possible. I was never given the opportunity to discuss alternatives to abortion, the potential side effects of abortion, or anything that could happen after the procedure.

It was like stepping into a rushing river that was pushing me through so fast that there was no opportunity to question or back out.

There was no mention of side effects at all. No mention that it could ruin my chances of ever conceiving a baby again. No mention that it could cause me to suffer from anxiety or depression. No mention that there would be any side effects; just go, go, get it done.

But I knew it had affected me. I knew I was sadder than I'd ever been. I knew that I didn't walk out of the abortion unscathed. I was so angry. The aftermath was just beginning to reveal its impact.

Are you dealing with anger and the aftermath? Take it all to God.

> *Nothing about me is hidden from you! I was secretly woven together out of human sight, but with Your own eyes you saw my body being formed. Even before I was born, you had written in your book everything about me.*
> -Psalm 139:16 (CEV)

Prayer
Dear God, Forgive me for listening to the current culture, and not listening to my intuition. Help me to let go of this anger once and for all.

Action
Pour out your heart to God on the journal pages, and tell Him how and in every way abortion has affected you.

Affirmation
I have confronted my anger and have let it go. I am patient and have self-control.

"Anger makes us feel so isolated."
–Fred Rogers

JOURNAL

Numb

I made the only choice I thought I had: I had an abortion. And I buried it deep, but it never went away. I took it with me everywhere I went. I secretly cringed on every abortion anniversary and privately grieved on what could have been the birthday. When thoughts of my abortion came into my head, I would ask God repeatedly to forgive me, and then I'd bury it again. I found myself going through the motions of life, but life seemed to have lost some of its color. I felt numb and detached.

I never stopped long enough to consider what could have caused this numbness. This detachment I felt from others and events that I would have normally been excited about. I never considered it had any connection to my abortion. In hindsight, looking at my timeline, it was obvious that it had a direct correlation since it began immediately after the abortion.

What's changed for you? Do you feel a little more pessimistic or critical than where you were before? Do you feel like the light in your eyes has dimmed just a little? Are your friends and loved ones at arm's length?

I was like all this and more. Then, one night, I felt compelled to pray to God. So, I got on my knees, and out of sheer hopelessness, I prayed the following prayer:

"God, I am so far from who you made me to be. Make me into who you intended me to be."

I spoke those words into the atmosphere without emotion or expression in my voice. Then I got up off my knees and went to sleep. I think God breathed a huge sigh of relief that I had finally asked for His help.

> *I am numb and completely devastated. I roar because my heart's in turmoil.*
> -Psalm 38:8 (GW)

Prayer

Dear God, You created everything with intention and purpose. Help me to be who you created me to be!

Action

Journal all the gifts and talents you have. Then, write a prayer, asking God to help you use them to a greater potential.

Affirmation

I'm letting go of everything that has held me down and using all my gifts and talents starting now.

"God knows our situation; He will not judge us as if we had no difficulties to overcome. What matters is the sincerity and perseverance of our will to overcome them."

-C.S. Lewis

JOURNAL

Triggers

Years of burying my abortion took a toll on me. The joyful, full-of-life person I once was became increasingly more of an act. I wasn't me anymore; I was angry, sad, and cynical all at the same time. It wasn't like I didn't enjoy life; I did, but there was an edge on me, a sharp edge that wasn't there before—a cynicism, for lack of a better way to say it.

Unknown to me at the time, I had many triggers that connected me back to my abortion. They caused unpredictable emotional reactions, like picking up a glass shard - instant pain!

A trigger is something that sparks a memory, an emotion, or a symptom that is related to past trauma. Triggers can spark intense emotional reactions. In my case, my triggers were related to babies, and specifically being around babies.

Family gatherings were a trigger for me. Friends having babies were a trigger. Baby showers were a trigger that could set me off into a rage or feelings of profound sadness. As a result, I would avoid anything that could set me off.

When I finally told my family about my abortion, my brother exclaimed, "That's it! Now I get it. That's why we had to walk on eggshells around you!" That was very eye-opening to me.

What are your triggers? Maybe, like me, you're ignoring your triggers? And don't say you don't have any because we all do. They could be waiting rooms, long hallways, feeling powerless, fear of others finding out, sounds, and the list goes on.

> Even when I walk through the darkest valley, I will not be afraid, for you are close beside me.
> -Psalm 23:4a (NLT)

Prayer

> Dear God, Help me recognize triggers that bring me back to emotional trauma in my life. And God, would you please heal that trauma?

Action

Write Triggers at the top of a page in your journal. When a trigger occurs, write it in your journal. Describe how you're feeling and coping. Knowing your triggers will help you be prepared ahead of time when they occur.

Affirmation

I am learning to recognize negative triggers in my life and to immediately ask God for help in not letting them bring me down.

"Some people feel the rain, others just get wet."
-Bob Dylan

JOURNAL

Wounded

Abortion wounded me. That's the truth. After I had an abortion, my outlook changed. My relationships changed; I pulled away from those I loved the most. My self-esteem was damaged.

Abortion is an ugly procedure. Removing the fetus from the mother is often done, taking one piece at a time. I won't go into those details, but just as my child was disassembled in my womb, so was my heart. It was shattered, and what was left was broken, sharp-edged pieces.

The psychological and physical consequences following abortion have long been neglected. We don't talk about the effects abortion has on the woman. If it were discussed, I believe many women would choose not to abort and consider the alternatives.

There are millions of women who, just like me, think, "I can do this, and it will be done," never anticipating any residual effects. But that is not the way we've been built. We've been built to carry our children all our lives.

There is scientific evidence that we carry them all our lives. It's called Fetal Microchimerism*, a biological phenomenon first discovered in the 1990s. It is a cellular connection between every mother and child created in her womb. Researchers discovered that the cells of children remain in the bodies of their mothers. These cells remain whether the child is born, miscarried, or aborted. Microchimerism has been recorded in many organs of the body, including the heart. Think about it: the cells of our children remain in our bodies. It brings truth to the words, "I carry you in my heart."

Research has also found that the fetal cells found in the mother will migrate to an injury and help to repair it. If the mother has a heart attack, those cells are the first to go to the area of injury to help. That blows my mind.

Have you questioned what you're feeling? Have you wondered why some thoughts and feelings have lingered?

He heals the wounds of every shattered heart.
-Psalm 147:3 (NLT)

Prayer

Dear God, I'm wounded too. And just like you did for Pam, would you heal my wounds as well? Thanks.

Action

Write a prayer in Your journal thanking God for healing your broken heart. The moment you asked God to heal your wounds, He went into action. It's a process, be patient, God isn't finished with you yet.

Affirmation

I have asked God to heal me, and the healing process has begun!

"Keep your face to the sunshine and you cannot see a shadow."

-Helen Keller

JOURNAL

_____

_____

_____

_____

_____

_____

_____

_____

Stuck

For years I felt stuck. I felt like nothing was ever going to change. I felt I was in an isolated place, and I couldn't move forward and I couldn't go back. I was constantly in fear of anyone getting too close.

I remember the day my family met at our favorite restaurant for dinner. There were about ten of us sitting at a long table. We were talking and laughing when my brother called to me from the other end of the table. "Hey, Pam, do you remember this song?" And he started to sing a song we knew from when we were young. The lyrics of the song went Hear the little heartbeat, see the forming image, what are you afraid of, can you drown the memories? That song was all about having an abortion.

I was in shock and terrified that my family would look at me at that moment and know that I had an abortion. That they'd look at me and know, and never look at me the same. I said, "Yeah, Dave, I remember it," and looked away. Thankfully, the conversation quickly turned to something else. But I didn't forget that song. The words to that song rang in my head for the following week, and little did I know it was that song that started the process of me getting unstuck.

Have you felt stuck? Like you've put yourself in a place you can't escape? Do you feel there's no help? That no one could possibly understand? God understands and loves you. He created you to know Him personally.

> *But whenever someone turns to the Lord, the veil is taken away. For the Lord is the Spirit, and wherever the Spirit of the Lord is, there is freedom.*
> -2 Corinthians 3:16-17 (NLT)

Pray this simple prayer:

Dear God, I turn to You and ask You to help me to get unstuck.

Action

Ask Jesus to come into your life by praying this prayer:

Dear Jesus, I believe that you are God's one and only son sent to die for the sins of all mankind. I believe God raised You from the dead, breaking all the power sin and death had over me. I accept You as my Saviour and Lord and ask You to forgive me of all my sins. Fill me with Your Spirit and restore me to the Father. I'm all Yours, Lord Jesus.

If you're not sure about accepting Jesus as your Lord and Saviour, don't worry, keep going.

Affirmation:

My old life is gone, and my new life has begun. I'm saved because Jesus saved me.

"Look for yourself, and you will find in the long run only hatred, loneliness, despair, rage, ruin, and decay. But look for Christ and you will find Him, and with Him everything else thrown in."

-C.S. Lewis, *Mere Christianity*

JOURNAL

_____

_____

_____

_____

_____

_____

_____

HEALING THE IMPOSSIBLE

Shame

Shame seemed like a shadow that I cast everywhere I went. Shame overwhelmed me the moment I realized I was pregnant. It constantly murmured in my head, "You're a loser; look what you've done; how did you get in this mess?; you know you can't tell anyone; they'll never look at you the same."

Shame told me I couldn't tell my parents because it would completely destroy the image they had of me. Shame told me I couldn't possibly tell my sisters; Cynthia is a nurse, and she might know negative effects of abortion, and Leslie was never able to have children, so I couldn't bring that sadness on her. And shame screamed at me, "You can't tell your brother Dave because he's a pastor, and you would bring shame on him."

So, the cycle of shame started and kept going around and around in my head, driving me deeper and deeper into condemnation, isolation, depression and darkness. But God!

One day, when I wasn't expecting it, God reached into that pit and pulled me out.

Are you dealing with shame? Has a darkness brought you into condemnation, isolation and despair? Let me just say there is no deep and dark place that God can not pull you out of.

> *So now there is no condemnation for those who belong to Christ Jesus.*
> -Romans 8:1 (NLT)

Prayer

Dear God, When I accepted Jesus as my Saviour and Lord, You threw my shame behind Your back, never to be thought of again. Thanks!

Action

Write this in your Journal: Those who look to Him will be radiant with joy; no shadow of shame will darken their faces. -Psalm 34:5

Now write the words: That's me!

Affirmation

I look to Jesus and am radiant with Joy; no shadow of shame is on me.

"When you're tempted to give up, your breakthrough is probably just around the corner."

- Joyce Meyer

JOURNAL

_____
_____
_____
_____
_____
_____
_____
_____
_____
_____
_____
_____
_____
_____
_____
_____
_____
_____
_____
_____

Premeditated

I chose to abort the moment I knew I was pregnant; I didn't entertain any thoughts in my head of carrying my child to term. How cold and callous it must sound now, but a negative voice in my head had convinced me that I had no other option.

I was listening to the voice of fear and shame, the voice of dread, voices from the pit. Fear overwhelmed me to the point that it stopped me from reaching out to others who could have helped me.

I tried to tell a friend once. She could have talked with me about it. Maybe it would have been good to have another perspective? But I decided against it at the last minute.

I went through with the abortion anyway. That negative voice had fully convinced me to do it, just get it done, like get out of my way. So, at that point, I was convinced to have an abortion, and nothing was going to stop me.

I never gave myself a moment to sit and think, and to ponder my decision. My only thoughts were to get it done. I didn't think about having a baby, just ending the pregnancy.

What I did was premeditated. How can God forgive me of that? Well, I don't know how, but he did. He forgave me the first time I asked with sincerity, and then he took it further and healed my heart.

Are you feeling cold or bitter? Bring it to God, lay it all at His feet, and ask for forgiveness.

> *For the wages of sin is death, but the free gift of God is eternal life in Christ Jesus our Lord.*
> *-Romans 6:23 (NLT)*

Prayer

Dear God, forgive me of my sins and thank You for forgiving me even when I thought what I did was unforgivable. Thank you!!!

Action

Write a prayer of thanksgiving to Father God on your journal pages. Here's a prompt:

Dear God, thank You for forgiving me, and ...

Affirmation

I confessed my sins to God, and He instantly forgave me and cleansed me from all my offenses.

"To be a Christian means to forgive the inexcusable, because God has forgiven the inexcusable in you."

-C.S. Lewis

JOURNAL

Guilt

Why was I still feeling so guilty? I thought, if I had asked God to forgive me, that would be it. He would forgive me, done and dusted. So why was I still feeling so guilty?

Then it dawned on me as the pieces began falling into place. As I battled with the guilt of what I had done, I began to realize that God was using guilt to bring it all into the light.

As long as I kept it all hidden, God wasn't able to deal with it and heal me. Once I brought it to God and asked for forgiveness and healing, God immediately went into action.

The negative voices used shame to bring me down, to shut me up, and to lock me up in a cage of condemnation and silence. But God! He used guilt not only to help me confess my sin and ask for forgiveness but also to bring it all into the light, out of hiding, so that He could help me. So He could heal me.

I had been running for so long away from God that when I asked for forgiveness, I realized He was right in front of me the whole time. He was right there with His arms open wide, waiting for me to fall into them, say sorry, and wrap me up in His love.

Have you been battling with guilt? Could it be that God is reminding you of something?

> *Paradoxically, my bitter experience was pushing me toward wholeness. For You, God, have put behind all my shortcomings and wrongdoings. You have rescued me from death. You pulled me from a black hole of nothingness and held me close to You.*
> -Isaiah 38:17 (VOICE)

Prayer

Dear God, Thank You for forgiving me of all my sins. Thank You for using guilt to bring me to You. Thank You for being right there, waiting for me.

Action

Pray and ask God to reveal what's hidden in your life that needs to be revealed so you can heal. Write down what comes to mind on a separate piece of paper, and then take it to God in prayer and ask for forgiveness. Now, take the piece of paper, tear it to shreds, and throw it away. Know that God hears your prayers and has sprung into action.

Affirmation

God has called me back to Him, saying, "You are mine, for I have chosen you.'

"Prayer doesn't just change situations; it also changes you."

-Anonymous

JOURNAL

_____
_____
_____
_____
_____
_____
_____
_____
_____
_____
_____
_____
_____
_____
_____

What If?

As much as I tried, I couldn't stop the What ifs.

Thoughts of "What If" kept rolling around in my mind. What if I didn't do it? Where would I be? What if I didn't do it? How old would my child be? What would they look like, what would they love? Would they have my big brown eyes?

I would try to turn off those thoughts as quickly as they came because they would bring a heaviness with them that I didn't want to deal with. All along, I hoped those thoughts would one day just go away. Thoughts I never expected I'd have. But they never did go away.

I don't know if every woman who chooses abortion stops to think about what could have been, but for me, I couldn't help but think of that from time to time.

Have you dealt with the what ifs? I don't believe anyone can go through life without confronting the what ifs at some point or another. I think they're rooted in regret, and has anyone ever lived a life where they've never experienced regret? No!

It's time to learn from the regret and the what ifs and let them go.

> *Pour out all your worries and stress upon him and leave them there, For He always tenderly cares for you.*
> -1 Peter 5:7 (TPT)

Prayer

Dear God, I give all my regrets and what-ifs and I leave them there with you. Help me to learn from them, make sense of them, and avoid future mistakes that could lead me back into them.

Action

Has anything good come out of your abortion experience? Write a statement of the good that has come from this, what you've learned, character building, and hope for the future.

Affirmation

Jesus Himself carried my sins in His body on the cross and now I am dead to sin and live authenticity.

"When we clear away our regrets, joy replaces resentment, and peace replaces conflict."
- Anonymous

JOURNAL

Grief

I was grieving in a way I never expected to grieve. I never saw it coming. I was grieving who I was. I was grieving the loss of a child I didn't know. I was grieving in ways I didn't understand. If I was so determined to have this abortion, why was I now dealing with feelings that seemed to have come out of nowhere?

No one told me the potential side effects abortion could have on me. Not a peep.

My heart ached. I felt empty and shallow like I had a big gaping wound that wouldn't heal, and yet no one knew.

I came to understand that what I was dealing with was disenfranchised grief.

Disenfranchised grief is a natural emotional reaction following a loss that is not openly accepted by society. And I don't have to tell you that abortion loss is not openly accepted, it's hardly acknowledged. Abortion loss, there are two words you don't see used together.

We're being made to believe the only emotion after an abortion is relief. Well, I can tell you firsthand, that's not true.

Somehow, I was dealing with a grief that I couldn't shake. Was this my body's natural reaction to the abortion loss?

No one else knew about it because I wasn't talking about it. I eventually took my grief to God, and He helped me, and He healed me.

Are you suffering feelings of grief and loss from your previous abortion(s)? There is hope. God promises to comfort those who mourn.

> *Blessed are those who mourn,*
> *for they will be comforted.*
> -Matthew 5:4 (NASB2020)

Prayer

Dear God, I never expected to have feelings of loss, and I never expected to grieve after I chose abortion. Thank you for forgiving me and comforting me in my grief.

Action

Write a description of what grief looks like to you. Then, give your grief to God and ask Him to heal your heart.

Affirmation

God is the strength of my heart and my portion forever.

"No one ever told me that grief felt so like fear."

-C.S. Lewis

JOURNAL

_____
_____
_____
_____
_____
_____
_____
_____
_____
_____
_____
_____
_____
_____
_____

God?

Why didn't God stop me? When I think about the path I chose, the decisions I've made, I can't help but think, why didn't God stop me? If God knew that my decision to abort would affect me so much, why didn't He step in and stop me?

God made us people of choice. We have free will to do whatever we like. That means we can choose to live our lives any way we choose. And we can choose to believe in Him or not.

When I found out I was pregnant, I didn't hesitate to make the decision to abort. I never thought twice about it. I never thought about God; He didn't even come to mind. I made my choice, even though a small voice whispered in my head, "Don't do it; you'll regret it."

So how can I, after the fact, dare to say "God, where were you?"

I know He was there all the time. He never left me. He only hoped I'd come to Him for help. But I never did; I just went straight and had an abortion.

Then, years later, after I had asked God to forgive me, I was reading my Bible, and I read these verses: "Bless the Lord, O my soul, and forget not all His benefits: Who forgives all your iniquities," Psalm 103:2-3a NKJV. I burst into tears and knew at that moment that God had forgiven me of the premeditated and deliberate sin of having an abortion.

Have you been blaming God for not stopping you? It wasn't His fault; He loves you..

> *You kissed my heart with forgiveness,*
> *in spite of all I've done.*
> -Psalm 103:3a (TPT)

Prayer

Dear God, Thank You for being there, for rescuing me, and forgiving me, and refreshing my life.

Action

Journal how you are feeling right now. Has anything changed since you began this book? What has changed?

Affirmation

I cried to God in my distress, He answered me and now I'm free from all my fears.

"Only God's presence can change people's lives."

-Priscilla Shirer

# JOURNAL

Ask

God didn't waste any time. When my friend Nancy prayed for me and told me I needed healing "when I was ready," I didn't realize how ready I was, but God did.

That same night, I went to a conference. Before it began, I checked out the bookstore. I walked into the large hall full of booths and books, and BAM! Right in front of me was a lady holding out a clipboard asking me if I'd like to complete a survey with a chance to win a prize. She was smiling and seemed very nice, so I took the clipboard, said "Sure," and began to fill it out.

It didn't take long for me to realize the survey was all about abortion. As I completed the survey, I looked over her shoulder and saw the name on her booth: "Abortion Recovery Centre." WHAT???!!!

It was just that morning that I had breakfast with Nancy. The same morning, Nancy prayed for me and told me I needed healing. God didn't waste any time, He wanted my healing to start that same day, and it did.

I finished the survey and completed the ballet to win a prize, and I knew then that I had taken the first step toward my healing.

> *And we are confident that He hears us whenever we ask for anything that pleases him.*
> *-1 John 5:14 (NLT)*

Prayer

Dear God, Thank You, for knowing what I need even before I even ask, and that You are always there ready to listen.

Action

Write a prayer to God of what you need today. He is waiting to hear from you.

Affirmation

God is a good Father and knows what I need before I ask. I will keep asking, seeking, and knocking.

"Don't bother to give God instructions, just report for duty." -
Corrie Ten Boom

JOURNAL

Courage

Sure enough, the Abortion Recovery Centre followed up with an email. I didn't win a prize, but they extended an offer of help.

I knew I had to call them. I was very reluctant to call but knew it was something I had to do if I wanted to heal and get over all this.

So, I called them, and that took guts. A bright cheery voice answered the phone. I told her that I was calling to follow up on the email I received. She suggested I book an appointment to talk with one of the peer counselors.

I agreed and told her I was only available on a certain day because I worked shift work. The cheery person checked the schedule and said, "I'm sorry we're completely booked that day," She asked if another day would work. I said "no," but before I could hang up, she said, "Hang on," and put me on hold.

I wanted to hang up. Everything in me wanted to end the call right then, but I couldn't do it to that cheery person. So, I stayed on hold and prayed, "God, if you can't get me in now, I'm not calling back. I'm good. Isn't this enough? I'm good."

In less than a minute, that Cheery voice came back online and said to me (like I just won a car), "I got you in!" So, I booked a one-on-one with a peer counselor, and ended up in a small group. It was a ten-week abortion recovery program. In the following months, I worked through each emotion. I prayed a lot, and God healed my brokenness. I'm so thankful I didn't hang up, but I held on.

Don't give up, hang on, and keep going!

> *And I find that the strength of Christ's explosive power infuses me to conquer every difficulty.*
> *- Philippians 4:13 (TPT)*

Prayer

Dear God, Thank You for never giving up on me.

Action

Write a letter to God telling Him all the reasons you're not giving up.

Affirmation

I won't give up; I will finish this book and finish well.

"Life is like riding a bicycle. To keep your balance, you must keep moving."

-Albert Einstein

JOURNAL

Forgiveness

Sin is like a mushroom; it resides and grows in the dark.

I had asked God to forgive me, and He forgave me, but I was still hurting.

By keeping it in the dark and not telling anyone, I wasn't getting the total healing I desperately needed. I needed to bring it out into the light so I could experience complete healing.

By acknowledging my sin of abortion to my friend Nancy, I was bringing it into the light. That allowed the Spirit of God to start work on restoring me.

When I came into the light and shared what I had done, not everyone understood or even agreed that what I had done was wrong. I knew in my heart that what I had done was wrong. Confessing it and getting if off my back was exactly what I needed to do.

Some people responded negatively to me, but I wasn't doing this for their approval. I was following what I knew I needed to do.

I encourage you to pray and ask God to show you where you can find help; people who genuinely care, understand, and will walk with you through your healing journey. I found help at abortionrecovery.ca.

> *Confess your sins to each other and pray for each other so that you may be healed. The earnest prayer of a righteous person has great power and produces wonderful results.*
> - James 5:16 (NLT)

Prayer

Dear God, Thank You for the way You brought me to a safe place to admit my sin. Thank You for leading me to people who genuinely care about me.

Action

What does a true friend look like to you? Write your description of a true friend in your journal. Then pray and ask God for a true friend and thank Him the ones He has already given you.

Affirmation

I confessed my sins, and God, in His mercy, forgave me; now I'm living a rich and full life!

"Just thinking about a friend makes you want to do a happy dance, because a friend is someone who loves you in spite of your faults."

-Charles Schulz

JOURNAL

Forgive

Somehow, I knew, I needed to forgive. I had this sense that forgiveness was a big part of my healing journey. I really didn't know where to start. There were so many people I was angry at regarding to my abortion.

Who was I angry at? I had to really think about that one. So I did, and one by one, it came to me who I needed to forgive. Before this, I had never sat down long enough to realize that I was angry and at whom I was angry.

Then came the hard part, which was forgiveness itself. How do I forgive? How do I forgive these people?

It wasn't easy. I didn't know how I was going to forgive them. So, I prayed something like this: "Dear God, I don't know how I'm going to forgive them. Please, help me to forgive; I can't do this without Your help." I just kept praying that prayer.

I didn't run to these people to say I forgive them. My forgiving them was just between me and God.

One day, a while later, I saw one of the people I needed to forgive. All the anger and bitterness I had once held against them was gone. It felt like a physical heaviness left my body, I knew that moment God had helped me forgive them.

I never did go to any of them to let them know I forgave them; somehow, I knew it wasn't necessary. I had forgiven them, and God was happy about that.

Forgiving others doesn't mean letting them off the hook for what they did to you. Forgiveness is letting go of the anger and setting yourself free.

> *Make allowance for each other's faults, and forgive anyone who offends you. Remember, the Lord forgave you, so you must forgive others.*
> -Colossians 3:13 (NLT)

Prayer

Dear God, Help me to know who I need to forgive, and help me to forgive them. I can't do this without Your help.

Action

Ask God who you need to forgive. Sit down and think about it. As God brings people to your mind, write their names in your journal in pencil. Then, take each one and ask God to help you forgive them. Go back and erase their names once you've forgiven them.

Affirmation

I forgive others because God forgave me. When I find it hard to forgive, Jesus helps me.

"Unforgiveness is like drinking poison and expecting the other person to die."

-Anonymous

JOURNAL

Forgive Myself

What about me? As I walked through the process of forgiving others, I ignored the glaring fact that I needed to forgive myself.

Forgiving others was hard, but this was harder. I think mainly because I had to come clean with my own actions; My part in all of this.

I wasn't an innocent party. I did my part to get myself into this mess and it was me who made the choice to abort.

I couldn't ignore it any longer. I had lived long enough with it hanging over my head. If God had forgiven me, why was I still beating myself up?

It was time to forgive myself. Let go of the past, leave it there, and walk into a brighter future.

So I asked God to help me to forgive myself. And He did, and I forgave myself.

So now the case is closed. there remains no accusing voice of condemnation against those who are joined in life-union with Jesus, the Anointed One.

- Romans 8:1 (TPT)

Prayer

Dear God, Thank You for showing me who I must forgive, including myself. And thank You for helping me and for forgiving me. Thank You that the past is now in the past.

Action

Write the following on your journal pages: "I can do everything through Christ, who gives me strength." That's found in the book of Philippians 4:13. Now write a list of all the things you'd like to do. Use your imagination, dream big, and write it all down.

Affirmation

I recognize when the enemy puts negative thoughts in my head, and I immediately take them captive and bring them to Jesus.

"There is a lioness within every one of God's daughters, and it is time that she awakens."

-Lisa Bevere

HEALING THE IMPOSSIBLE

JOURNAL

Hello

"This week's assignment is to pray and ask God what the gender of your child is," said one of the leaders in my Abortion Recovery Group. What? The question stopped me in my tracks as I felt my hands clench my book tighter. I swallowed hard as I choked out my reply. "Ok, sounds good," I said with a forced smile.

It didn't sound good to me one bit. It sounded unnerving, and I didn't want to do the assignment. Couldn't we just leave it where it was? This 'healing journey' was going too far, too deep. But I was obedient and prayed a simple prayer; "God, would you please reveal the gender of my child?"

I didn't get an answer right away. But, just before waking up, I had a dream one morning. I watched a little girl running through a beautiful field in my dream. Her hair was flowing in the wind, and the flowers on her dress seemed to float up and off her dress and up as she ran.

Then I looked at where she was running and saw my father, who had died several years before. He was grinning from ear to ear, with his arms open wide. I watched as she leaped into my Dad's arms. He swooped her up and gently sat down, placing this beautiful little child on his lap. Then I woke up.

I knew then that God had shown me in a dream that I had a daughter and that my daughter was in heaven.

> *But Jesus said, "Let the children come to me. Don't stop them! For the Kingdom of Heaven belongs to those who are like these children.*
> *-Matthew 19:14 (NLT)*

Prayer

Dear God, Would you please reveal the gender of my child to me?

Action

Keep praying for God to reveal your child. When He does, write it in your journal. Then pray and ask God, what their name is. My daughter's name is Priscilla (which I've shortened to Sylla), named after my Grandmother.

Affirmation

God is a good Father, and He loves me with an everlasting love.

> "Sometimes the smallest things take up the most room in our hearts."
>
> -Winnie the Pooh

JOURNAL

_____
_____
_____
_____
_____
_____
_____
_____
_____
_____
_____
_____
_____
_____
_____
_____

Heaven

I was with my Mom when she passed from this life to the next. I couldn't begin to describe the profound peace I sensed in her room that day.

The care home called me and told me to come right away, that my Mom's breathing had changed. I sped all the way there and ran into her room. Somehow, I knew in my heart this was it.

I gently held her head in my hands and said, "Mom, I'm here." She was in a deep sleep but managed to open her eyes for a fraction of a second and smile. She knew I was there. I held my Mom's hand, stroked her hair, told her I loved her and listened as she breathed deeply.

As I sat beside my Mom, I listened to each breath as they came further and further apart. Then she took her last breath, and she was gone.

A few days later, I prayed and asked God if I could get a glimpse of Mom in heaven, and in a dream one early morning, this is what I saw:

I saw a vast group of people all bathed in white light. I couldn't see faces, but in the middle and slightly ahead of the group, I knew it was Jesus. And the light was coming from Him. Somehow, I also knew my Dad was beside Jesus, to His right. I could sense they were waiting for an arrival.

My perspective changed from being in front of this vast crowd to being beside my Dad. He had his hands on the shoulders of a little girl. Then he leaned down, and I heard him say to the little girl, "That's her," and he gave her a gentle nudge.

Immediately I was back beside who I knew now was my Mom. She was arriving in heaven, and a huge crowd awaited her arrival. I saw the little girl run up to my Mom, lifting her arms up to her, as she said "Grandma!" My Mom bent down to pick her up. Then I woke up.

God, in His infinite love, gave me more than I had asked for. He gave me (what I believe was) a small glimpse of my Mom's arrival in heaven. God answered my prayer, gave me a hint of heaven, and healed my broken heart over my Mom's passing. God is real; heaven is a real place. I'm going there one day.

No eye has seen, no ear has heard, and no mind has imagined what God has prepared for those who love him.

- 1 Corinthians 2:9 (NLT)

Prayer

Dear God, Thank You that one day, I will see my child(ren) again.

Action

Journal a prayer about heaven.

Affirmation

I have made Jesus my Lord and Saviour, and know I'll live forever with Him!

"Real people and real relationships do not end when this life ends, they go on to new depths."
-John Burke

JOURNAL

_____

_____

_____

_____

_____

_____

_____

_____

_____

Letter

Where do you mail a letter to Heaven? I was challenged by my facilitators in the abortion recovery group to write a letter to my child in heaven.

I struggled with this because the thought of her still brought sadness. But, it was more than just sadness; I had to come face to face with the fact that I was a mother. That was harder to grasp; however, writing a letter to my daughter Sylla helped.

It was uncomfortable at first, but as I began to write, my letter began to flow. Here's part of what I wrote:

> *Dear Silla,*
> *I am longing to see you and be reunited with you and all my loved ones who have passed on. I am sad that I took the life God had planned away from you. God has forgiven me, blotted out my sins, and cast them into the sea of forgetfulness. That's from Micah 7:19. I love that verse. Now, I wait with*

great anticipation to one day see you and hold you in my arms. I still have a lot of work to do here, but one day we'll be together forever.
Love, your Mama

Now, you guessed it. I want to challenge you to do the same. Imagine your child sitting beside you, and they put their little hand in yours. Now, imagine what you would like to say to your child.

> *But why should I fast when he is dead? Can I bring him back again? I will go to him one day, but he cannot return to me.*
> -2 Samuel 12:23 (NLT)

Prayer

Dear God, Thank You for the assurance that my child is in heaven with You. Help me to write a letter that perfectly expresses my heart to my child.

Action

Write the letter to your child in the pages of your journal.

Affirmation

Because I have put my trust in Jesus, I know I'll see my child(ren) again.

"Maybe the reason we never feel fully satisfied in this life is because we were created for the life to come."

-John Burke

JOURNAL

Mail

Fullness of joy. Think about that statement for a minute.

Fullness means completeness, saturation, totality, and wholeness

Joy means bliss, comfort, delight, elation, satisfaction and wonder

Think about a time you felt joyful. Now imagine what fullness of joy could be.

It must be joy beyond anything we've ever experienced.

In heaven, there is fullness of joy. There is no sorrow, remorse, anger, or regret, just pure love and joy. No eye has seen, no ear has heard, and no mind has imagined what God has prepared for those who love him. That's a promise found in 1 Corinthians 2:9.

Take a few minutes to imagine your child in heaven. You shared your heart with your child; now imagine what your child wants to say to you. To help you get started, below is an excerpt of the letter I imagined my child wrote back to me.

Dear Mama,
You're my Mama, and we have a special bond. Even though we never got to be together, we have a special bond. I know you carry me with you in your heart, just as I carry you in mine.
I can't wait to run and jump into your arms.
Love, Sylla

You will show me the path of life: In Your presence is fullness of joy; at Your right hand are pleasures forevermore.
-Psalm 16:11 (NKJV)

Prayer

Dear God, Thank You for the promise of heaven. Thank You for everything You are preparing for those of us who love you. And thank You that one day I'll be reunited with my child/children in heaven.

Action

Write your letter from your child (or children) in heaven to you.

Affirmation

I love and trust God even though I have never seen Him and He rewards me with eternal life because I trust Him.

"Fill your paper with the breathings of your heart."

-William Woodsworth

JOURNAL

Grace

Grace is receiving what you don't deserve. Mercy is not receiving what we do deserve.

How could God possibly make good of what I had done? I had hidden my sin of abortion for over 20 years! For 20 years, an opposing force had me trapped in fear and condemnation. What a colossal waste of time.

God promises to bless us abundantly, and to pay us back for what the enemy has stole. So, I made that my prayer.

God made good on His promise and He gave me a family! I married a wonderful man with three adult children and a daughter-in-law. Since we've been married we gained another daughter-in-law and three gorgeous grandsons! God made me a wife, a mom, and a mother-in-law, and now I'm a grandma!

I am living proof of the amazing grace of God!

It's true; God gives you more than you could ever think or imagine!

To give them beauty for ashes, The oil of joy for mourning, The garment of praise for the spirit of heaviness; That they may be called trees of righteousness, The planting of the Lord, that He may be glorified."
-Isaiah 61: 3 (NKJV)

Prayer

Dear God, Thank You for taking the ashes of my life, and turning them into beauty. Thank You for giving me grace.

Action

Write this in your journal:

God can do far more than I could ever imagine in my wildest dreams! Dear God, here's a BIG audacious prayer...

Affirmation

God has given me joy where there was mourning and beauty where there were ashes. I am a light for Jesus in this dark world.

"Grace means that all of your mistakes now serve a purpose instead of serving shame".
-Anonymous

HEALING THE IMPOSSIBLE

JOURNAL

Hope

I hadn't experienced real hope for a long time. When I completed my abortion recovery group, I was filled with hope. Real Hope. Not just hope for my next trip or a promotion. Real hope. The kind that makes your life worth living.

All the baggage I had carried for so long was gone without a trace.

I knew I was forgiven.

My Mom had given me a Bible a year after my Father died. I had hardly cracked it open up to this point, but now I couldn't put it down.

I began to read the Bible daily. I also began to journal my thoughts as I read. I wanted to read the whole Bible in a year and so I did.

God had forgiven, restored, and filled me with hope for the future.

> *For I know the plans that I have for you, 'declares the LORD,' plans for prosperity and not for disaster, to give you a future and a hope.*
> -Jeremiah 29:11 (NASB2020)

Prayer

> Dear God, Thank You for restoring my life and filling me with hope. Give me a passion to read Your Word daily.

Action

Start reading the Bible every day. Buy one online or go to your nearest bookstore; they'll likely have one. There are many versions and I prefer the NLT – New Living Translation. It's an easy read. Start by reading the book of John in the New Testament. Then read a Psalm and a Proverb daily in the Old Testament, and in the New Testament begin in Matthew and continue reading until you finish, then begin again.

Affirmation

> In Jesus, I have a future, and my hope will never be cut off again.

> "When God forgives, He at once restores."
> -Theodore Epp

HEALING THE IMPOSSIBLE

JOURNAL

Purpose

Some people are born knowing exactly what they are to do in life. That certainly wasn't me. Well, I knew I wanted to travel the world, but as for a career? My career seemed less important and more of a means to an end. My job would pay for my travel.

I never consulted with God as to what He wanted me to do. When I applied for jobs, I would pray like mad that I would get them and then thank God when I did.

I never considered what God might want me to do. He seldom came into my thoughts. Suffice it to say, I never asked God directly what He wanted me to do with my life.

After going through the Abortion Recover Program, that all changed. As I started to read the Bible daily, I realized that God had plans and a purpose for my life. I could see how He had led me to various jobs and what He had taught me through them.

Now things were different. Now, I wanted to know exactly what God wanted me to do. I wanted to do all the things that He had created me to do. I was done wasting time and wanted to get right at it.

So, I took it all to Him and prayed. I asked God what my life purpose was and what He wanted me to do next.

> *For we are God's masterpiece. He has created us anew in Christ Jesus, so we can do the good things he planned for us long ago.*
> *– Ephesians 2:10 (NLT)*

Prayer

Dear God, Before I was born, You wrote plans of what You wanted me to do in my life. Would You please show me what you want me to do with my life? How can I put all the gifts and talents You gave me into action today?

Action

After you pray the prayer above, sit and listen for what God is saying; what words and images are coming into your mind. Record them in your journal and pray over them daily.

Affirmation

I trust in the Lord with all my heart, and don't lean on my own understanding. Every morning, I seek God's will in all I do, and He shows me which path to take.

"View yourself as a precious vessel He crafted for a unique purpose."

-Patricia Ennis

JOURNAL

Share

When God healed me I wanted to share it with the world. I was so thankful and thrilled for what God had done for me that I wanted to tell the world and tell them now! I knew there were other abortion-wounded women like me out there, and I wanted them to get the help I found.

The facilitator of my recovery group pulled my reins back and said, "Before you share with the world, you need to tell your family." She then encouraged me to pray and ask God who I should share my story with and when was the right time to share.

I knew right away God was prompting me to share my story with my family. I was eager to share it with my siblings, but the thought of telling my Mom was terrifying. Not because she'd be mad, actually the opposite, that she would be sad to have lost a grandchild.

I told my siblings, and they wrapped their arms around me and just loved me. It was awesome.

Then, about a week later, I broke the news to my Mom. As I had anticipated, it was hard. I'd say it was the hardest thing I've ever done. Mom was in shock and sad. Sad that she lost a grandchild, sad that I made that choice, and sad that she wasn't there for me.

Sharing with others can be hard. Pray about who God wants you to share your story with. Wait for His prompts to share and listen to Him when He tells you not to share.

> *Go home and tell your friends and tell them how much the Lord has done for you, and how he has had mercy on you.*
> -Mark 5:19b (ESV)

Prayer

Dear God, Who do you want me to share my story with? Give me the patience to wait on You, and give me an open door and the words when You want me to share my story.

Action

Write your story of what God has done for you. Consider starting with "I started on this journey feeling..."

And ending it with "Now I feel hope and..."

Affirmation

I sought the Lord, and He answered me and delivered me from all my fear, pain, and shame.

"One day you will tell your story of how you overcame what you went through and it will be someone else's survival guide."
–Anonymous

JOURNAL

_____
_____
_____
_____
_____
_____
_____
_____
_____
_____
_____
_____
_____

New Life

"Take off the grave cloths and let her go."

For years, I had hidden my secret of having an abortion, and for years I lived in fear that someone would find out. I was even fearful that I would somehow give it away myself.

Years of burying my abortion took a toll on me, and I was living bound in shame and sorrow.

There is a story in the Bible about a man named Lazarus. He was a friend of Jesus, and one day, Lazarus died. When Jesus arrived, Lazarus had been dead for three days. Jesus called to Lazarus to come out of the tomb. Lazarus came out of the tomb alive.

Jesus had raised him from being dead. Jesus said to the people around Lazarus, "Take off the grave cloths and let him go"

That's what it felt like to me that morning with Nancy. Following the Spirit of God's leading, she asked me, "What's the block, Pam?" Jesus was calling me out of the grave.

Then when He led me to the Abortion Recovery Centre, it was like He told them "Take off her grave clothes and let her go."

Just like the story of Lazarus in the Bible, Jesus came and raised me from being dead. I came out of the tomb that day, and Jesus started the process of unraveling all my grave clothes, everything that held me down.

There is a Chris Tomlin song that goes, "My chains are gone, I've been set free, My God, my Savior has ransomed me, And like a flood His mercy reigns, Unending love, amazing grace."

> *Jesus said to them, "Take off the grave clothes and let him go."*
> -John 11:44b (NIV)

Prayer

Dear God, Thank You for freeing me from my sin and shame. Help me to help others who are where I once was.

Action

Listen to Chris Tomlin's song: Amazing Grace (My Chains Are Gone) on your favorite music streaming service. Listen to it a few times and then write the lyrics in your journal.

Affirmation

I Praise God for comforting me in my troubles. He is now equipping me to comfort others with the same comfort I received from Him.

"There is an amazing and refreshing journey of freedom for those who know Jesus Christ as Lord."

-Crystal McDowell

JOURNAL

Pursue

God is in pursuit of you!

The very fact that you're holding this book is evidence of God's pursuit of you. He loves you with everlasting love and calls you to come to Him to be a part of His family.

God's love for us is so indescribable that He sent His one and only son to die for our sins. How He was resurrected from the dead and broke all the power sin and death had on us. You can be part of the family of God by believing in Jesus. He came, died for our sins, and was resurrected from the dead, breaking the power that sin and death held over us.

Pray with a sincere heart and ask Jesus to come into your heart and life as your Saviour.

I know this might sound repetitive, but there may be someone out there who has yet to believe. If that's you, take that step right now.

> *But to all who believed him and accepted him, he gave the right to become children of God. They are reborn—not with a physical birth resulting from human passion or plan, but a birth that comes from God.*
> - John 1:12-13 (NLT)

Prayer

Dear Jesus, I believe that you are God's one and only Son, that You lived a sinless life and died for the sins of mankind. I believe that Your sacrifice was how I could be restored to the right relationship with Father God. I repent for all my sins and thank You for forgiving me. I accept Your gift of forgiveness and eternal life. Thank You for saving me and placing me in the family of God.

Action

If you accepted Jesus as your Saviour today, record it in your journal. If you've been a Christ follower for a longer period of time, write a reflection of when you accepted Jesus as your Saviour.

Affirmation

I have accepted Jesus as my Lord and Saviour and am a new creation! The old me is gone, and the new me has begun! Thank You Jesus!

"Remember who you are. Don't compromise for anyone, for any reason. You are a child of the Almighty God. Live that truth."

-Lysa Terkeurst

JOURNAL

Thankful

When I look back and see where I was and where God has brought me, I can't help but thank Him and praise Him. He has given me a new life, hope, and future, and I am excited for what He has next for me.

> *Oh give thanks to the LORD, for he is good; for his steadfast love endures forever!*
> *-Psalm 118:1 (ESV)*

Prayer

Dear God, Thank You Father for everything. Thank You for not leaving me where I was and for taking me out of the pit, cleaning me off, and putting a new song in my heart to sing. Thank You for healing my broken heart. Thank You for sending Your Son Jesus to die for my sins and for the assurance that I will spend eternity with You and my child(ren). Thank You for turning my sorrow into Joy. Thank You for setting me free and for an amazing life, a future full of hope, and an eternity in Your presence!

Action

Write a list of twenty-five things or more of what you are thankful for. Then, leave some room to keep adding to your list.

Affirmation

I give thanks to God, for He makes everything right in the end. I sing my highest praise to God in the Highest Place!

"Gratitude makes sense of our past, brings peace for today, and creates a vision for tomorrow."

-Melody Beattie

JOURNAL

_____
_____
_____
_____
_____
_____

Restoration

I answered the phone; the voice was frantic and said, "They're working on him; they're working on him!" It was my Mom, and I knew she was talking about my Dad. I said, "I'm on my way, Mom," hung up, turned to my friend Janice, and said, "We got to go now." We were in Janice's car, flying down the street and heading to my parent's home, about 15 minutes away, in a matter of seconds. I said, "Pray, Janice, pray!" She fervently replied, "I am praying!"

At that moment, God spoke to my heart. His words were clear as a bell, "It's ok Pam, it's out of your control: this is the beginning of a process."

My Dad had a heart attack that night, and in the ten days that followed, our family sat a vigil with him until he took his last breath. We were all so heartbroken that Dad was gone; I cried buckets of tears, but I knew in my heart that it was "ok." God had already told me it was.

What a curious thing God said to me that night: "This is the beginning of a process." What did God mean by that? It took me years to unpack what He said to me that night.

God is a God of structure and process. He has a plan and purpose for our lives, and He works to bring us into our destiny. We can choose to align with Him or go out on our own.

Reading this book has been a process. By praying the prayers, journaling, and decreeing the affirmations, God has already begun the restoration work needed in your life. It's a process.

> *I am sprinting toward the only goal that counts: to cross the line, to win the prize, and to hear God's call to resurrection life found exclusively in Jesus the Anointed.*
> *–Philippians 3:14 (The VOICE)*

Prayer

> *Dear God, thank You for the restoration work You have already begun in my life. I align with Your will, so help me learn as I go. Thank You for promising to complete the work You start.*

Action

Write in your journal things you see God restoring in your life.

Decree

God causes all things to work together for good in my life because I love God, and He's called me to the destiny He wants for me, and I said yes!

"Your Destiny is chosen by God, your future is certain, whether you arrive there is up to you."

–Myles Munroe

JOURNAL

_____
_____
_____
_____
_____
_____
_____
_____
_____
_____
_____

Afterword
God Is Our Natural Environment

When God wanted to create fish, He spoke to the sea.

When God wanted to create trees, He spoke to the earth.

When God wanted to create us, He spoke to Himself.

What happens when we take a fish out of the sea? It dies.

What happens when you take a tree out of the soil? It dies.

What happens when we become disconnected from God? We die.

God is our natural environment. We were created to live in the presence of God. It is only in Him that life exists.

When Adam ruined it for the rest of us, God planned to get us back into the right relationship with Him. His plan was Jesus! To send his only son, Jesus, to take the blame and be the sacrifice for our sins. Jesus lived a sinless life. making Him the perfect and only possible sacrifice.

Life is in the blood, and Jesus shed His blood for our sins.

When God raised Jesus from the dead, it broke all the power that sin and death had over us.

Now that we have accepted Jesus as our personal Savior, God gives us eternal life with Him, saving us from the grave and hell.

> *"If you openly declare that Jesus is Lord and believe in your heart that God raised him from the dead, you will be saved."*
> - Romans 10:9 (NLT)

"I have never known anyone to accept Christ's redemption and later regret it." –C.S. Lewis

Now that you've begun your healing journey, don't stop here.

I encourage you to seek additional help and find your community. Remember, it's a process.

> "God can't give us peace and happiness apart from Himself because there is no such thing." -C.S. Lewis

You can find Pam at her website:

healingtheabortionwounded.com

Journal Prompts

As I begin my personal healing journey, I am feeling...

The thing that made me pick up this book was...

When I have completed this journey, I want to feel...

I need healing in the following ways...

My perfect day looks like this...

Who has influenced me the most in my morals and values? How did they affect me?

What biases do I hold?

What biases do I hold towards God and people?

How did having an abortion affect my heart?

How did having an abortion affect my mind?

How did having an abortion affect my studies?

How did having an abortion affect my long-term outlook?

Here is a list of all the talents I have...

Here's a list of things I'd like to learn...

What are triggers?

What are my triggers?

I am thankful for...

Dear God, thank you for forgiving me and...

What are some areas I tend to neglect in my life?

What are things I need to address in my life?

What have I learned from my abortion? Good and bad?

How am I feeling right now?

What, if anything, has changed since I began this book?

Is there anything or anyone that I am grieving over?

What are the biggest things I need God to do in my life?

What is my BHAP – Big Harry Audacious Prayer?

I am thankful for...

What makes me happy is...

What does a true friend look like to me?

Who do I need to forgive?

Who do I need to ask for forgiveness?

What are things I'd like to do that I've not done before?

What does the perfect day in heaven look like?

If I could do anything, I would...

What are more things for which I am thankful?

What is my most treasured memory?

What is my most treasured possession?

What kind of friend am I?

What kind of friend would l like to be?

What are some things I'd like to stop doing?

What are some things I'd like to start doing?

What are some of my best habits?

When I was a child, I imagined my life to be...

What is different in my adult life than I imagined life would be?

What could I do today to make my life better?

What is my biggest dream or life goal?

What do I need to do today to make that happen?

How would I describe the most beautiful place I've ever been to someone blind?

My favorite time of day is…

What makes me laugh?

What makes me cry?

What makes me feel all warm inside?

Why is it important to be honest?

If I could go anywhere, I'd go…

My description of a perfect day is…

Acknowledgments

Many people have helped me in my healing journey, but my deepest gratitude goes to my family. To the love of my life and the man of my dreams, Clay: Thank you for your love, wisdom, and constant support; And to the children God gave me: Dave, Angie, Malcolm, Alyssa, Ben, Kate, William, and Alexander. And to my sisters Cynthia and Leslie and my cousin Connie.

To my friend Nancy, thank you for getting me on the path to healing and restoration.

Thank you to my friend Stella, who continually challenges me and who challenged me to write a book to help other women who were wounded like me.

Thanks to Karen and Linda at ARC and Leah, who kept me laughing through the challenging Abortion Recover Program. And thanks, Debbie and Jasmine, and to all the "Jewels in His Crown": Fern, Lillian, Kat, Lauren, Colleen, and Melissa to name a few.

Thank you to my dear friends Marvin and Elinor for their love, support, and prayers. Also, thank you, Marvin and Stefanie, for helping me with editing and grammar.

Thank you to my heart friend Tina, and to Stephanie, Lori, Kristi, Julie, Ramona, and Anne. And thanks to my KHA girls Angela and Anjali. And all my friends who pray for me.

A heartfelt thank you to my oldest and dearest friends, Janice and Barb—the Ja and Ba of Pajaba. I'm so grateful for the incredible friendship God has blessed us with. You've loved me through life's ups and downs. Love you both! Pajaba forever!

To you, the reader, I hope this book inspires you to seek God and embrace all the amazing plans He has for you.

References

Page Five, How to use this book: *2018 Online Positive Affect Journaling in the Improvement of Mental Distress and Well-Being in General Medical Patients With Elevated Anxiety Symptoms: A Preliminary Randomized Controlled Trial

Chapter Eight: WOUNDED: Fetal microchimerism and maternal health: a review of evolutionary analysis of cooperation and conflict beyond the womb. By Amy M Boddy, Angelo Fortunato, Melissa Wilson Sayres, Athena Aktipis

AFFIRMATION REFERENCES
1. Block (John 14:27)
2. Shock (John 14:27, Isaiah 26:3)
3. Relief (Deuteronomy 31:8)
4. Memory (Psalm 30:2)
5. Anger (Proverbs 16:32)
6. Numb (Ephesians 4:31-32, Romans 12:6)

7. Triggers (Psalm 34:4)
8. Wounded (Mark 5:34)
9. STUCK (2 Corinthians 5:17)
10. Shame (Psalm 34:5)
11. Premeditated (1John 1:9)
12. Guilt (Isaiah 41:9-10)
13. What if (1 Peter 2:24)
14. Grief (Psalm 73:26)
15. God (Psalm 34:4)
16. Ask (1 John 5:14, Matthew 7:7-8)
17. Courage (Hebrews 10:35-36)
18. Forgiveness (Proverbs 28:13, John 10:10)
19. Forgive (Ephesians 4:32)
20. Forgive myself (2 Corinthians 10:5)
21. Hello (James 1:17, Jeremiah 31:3)
22. Heaven (John 3:16)
23. Letter (1 John 5:11)
24. Mail (1:Peter 1:8-9)
25. Grace (Isaiah 61:3, Matthew 5:14, Ephesians 3:20)
26. Hope (Proverbs 23:18)
27. Purpose (Proverbs 3:5-6)
28. Share (Psalm 34:4-7)
29. New Life (2 Corinthians 1:4)
30. Pursue (2 Corinthians 5:17)
31. Thankful (Psalm 7:17)
32. Restoration (Romans 8:28)

About the Author

Pam is devoted to truth. Having been wounded by abortion, Pam faced the reality and consequences of her decision and sought God for His forgiveness, and He restored her.

Pam now speaks and writes about what God has done in her life and what He can do in yours.

Pam is a deeply compassionate person who boldly proclaims the truth in a nonjudgemental and loving way.

Printed in the USA
CPSIA information can be obtained
at www.ICGtesting.com
CBHW051638101124
17132CB00005B/15